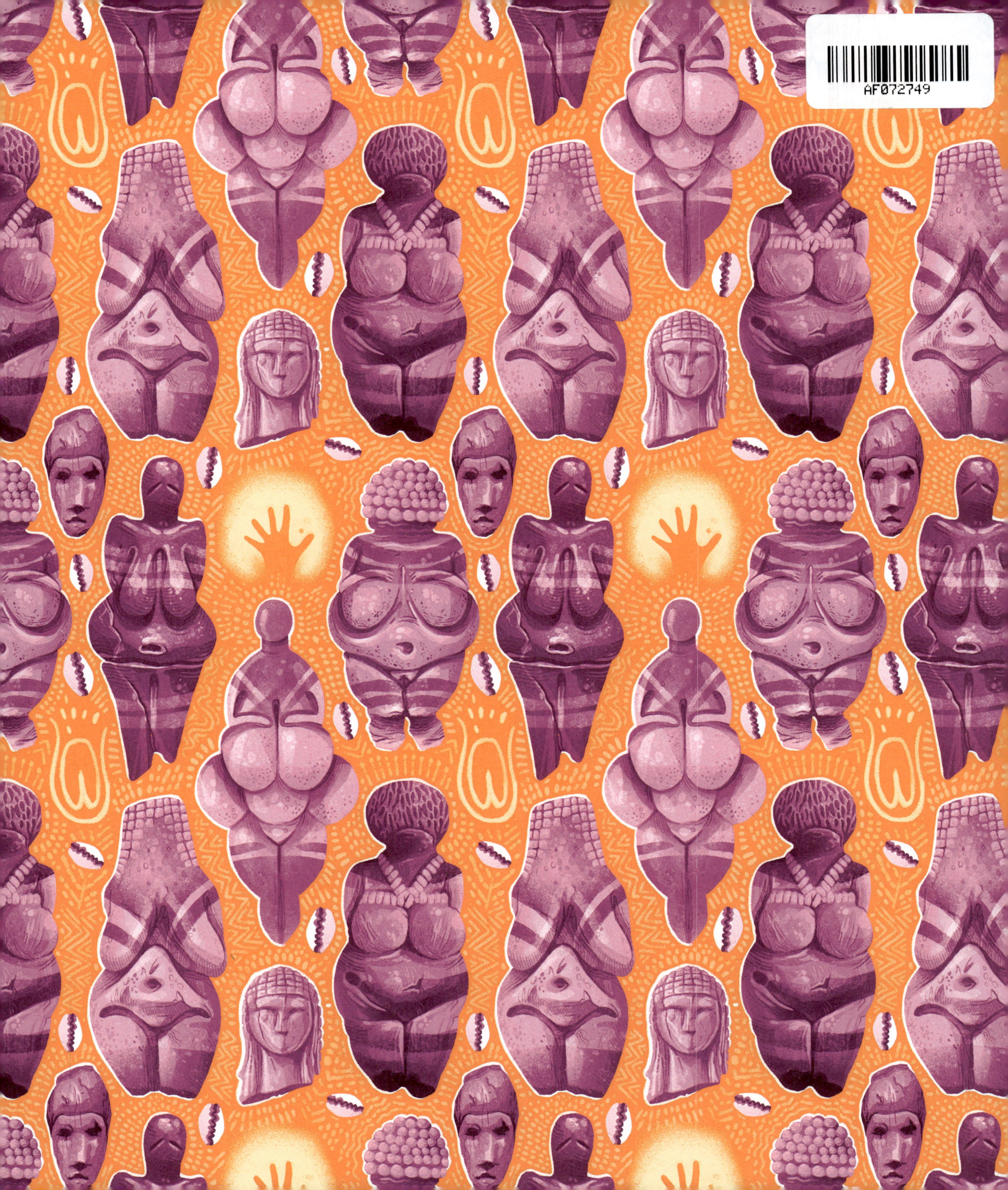

To the women in my life: beautiful, strong and brave. And with love to my
nieces Martina and Iria, I'll be at your side with every step you take.
MARTA

To all the young scientists and historians who work hard every day,
dedicating their lives to the subject they're passionate about. And to
everyone who supported my huge love for prehistory: I love you all so much.
DIEGO

The contents of this book have been checked and approved by the
Catalan Institute of Human Paleoecology and Social Evolution (IPHES).

To find out more about the archaelogical finds illustrated in this
book, try an internet search for the catalogue number of the fossil,
which is listed next to the image, e.g. KNM-WT 15000.

Translated from the Spanish *Femina sapiens*

First published in the United Kingdom in 2025 by
Thames & Hudson Ltd, 181A High Holborn, London WC1V 7QX

Original edition © 2024 Mosquito Books, Barcelona
Text © 2024 Marta Yustos
Illustrations © 2024 Diego Rodríguez Robredo
This edition © 2025 Thames & Hudson Ltd, London

All Rights Reserved. No part of this publication may be reproduced or transmitted in any form or
by any means, electronic or mechanical, including photocopy, recording, or any other information
storage and retrieval system, without prior permission in writing from the publisher.

British Library Cataloguing-in-Publication Data.
A catalogue record for this book is available from the British Library

ISBN 978-0-500-65389-0

Impression 01

Printed in Spain

Be the first to know about our new releases,
exclusive content and author events by visiting
thamesandhudson.com
thamesandhudsonusa.com
thamesandhudson.com.au

Marta Yustos
Diego Rodríguez Robredo

FEMINA SAPIENS®

Human evolution
and our female ancestors

TABLE OF CONTENTS

10 An Ancient Family Tree

12 Anatomy Lessons

14 Where It All Began

16 Standing Tall

18 Adapt or Die

40 Settled Lives

42 Inspiring Women

44 Our Family Album

38 Beyond Death

GLOSSARY

A list of some of the useful terms that appear in this book.

Archaeology The study of human history by finding and analysing the traces left behind by different societies.

Bipeds Animals that can walk on their two rear limbs. This sets them apart from quadrupeds, which walk on four legs.

DNA Short for deoxyribonucleic acid, a molecule that contains the genetic codes that all living things need in order to grow and develop.

Flint A hard stone made mostly of silica. When broken, it forms flakes with very sharp edges.

Fossil The remains or traces of a living thing that have been preserved in stone over a period of many thousands of years.

Genetics The study of how biological information is passed from one generation to another, through DNA.

Genus A group of living things in taxonomy, which can be divided into multiple species.

Handaxe A stone tool, made of flint or quarzite and shaped on both sides. Its form may be teardrop, triangular or rectangular. Its two cutting edges meet at the topmost point.

Hominids The group of great apes, which includes humans, gorillas, chimpanzees and orangutans, and their extinct ancestors.

Hominins A group of hominids that walk on two feet and stand upright. This includes modern humans and our immediate ancestors.

Ice age A long period in which the world's temperatures fall, causing glaciers and polar caps to spread and ice sheets to form.

Ochre An earth-based mineral, often yellow or red, which can be used as a pigment.

Palaeontologist Someone who studies fossils.

Quartzite A hard metamorphic rock made of interlocking layers of quartz crystals.

Species In taxonomy, a group of living things that are able to reproduce with each other and have fertile offspring.

Taxonomy The system of categories that scientists use to help them understand how all living things are related to each other. The image opposite shows which of these categories humans belong to.

A WINDOW ON THE PAST

Reconstructing the past is a bit like trying to put together a huge jigsaw puzzle, with many pieces that are either missing or broken. But with patience and hard work, people who study fossils are trying to complete this enormous puzzle and reveal the true story of human evolution.

This book is like a family album that shows who your many-times-great-grandmothers and grandfathers were. Its pages will open a window on the past that you can use to explore our origins and understand how humans came to exist and what life might have been life long ago, way before there were things like phones, electricity, supermarkets or cars.

There's also something unique about this adventure. When the study of archaeology began, it was, like many other sciences and disciplines, only done by men. Lots of male archaeologists, scientists and prehistorians have studied the past and made breathtaking discoveries. They were the ones who first wrote the story of human evolution, but that story was not always correct.

But what if the story of human evolution was told by our female ancestors instead? In this book we'll journey into prehistory to discover the different human species that came before us and put a face to the key players in our long evolutionary history. So fasten your seatbelts, because our long journey begins here.

Kingdom: Animal
Phylum: Chordata
Class: Mammalia
Order: Primates
Superfamily: Hominoidea
Family: Hominidae
Tribe: Hominini
Subtribe: Hominina
Genus: *Homo*
Species: *Homo sapiens*

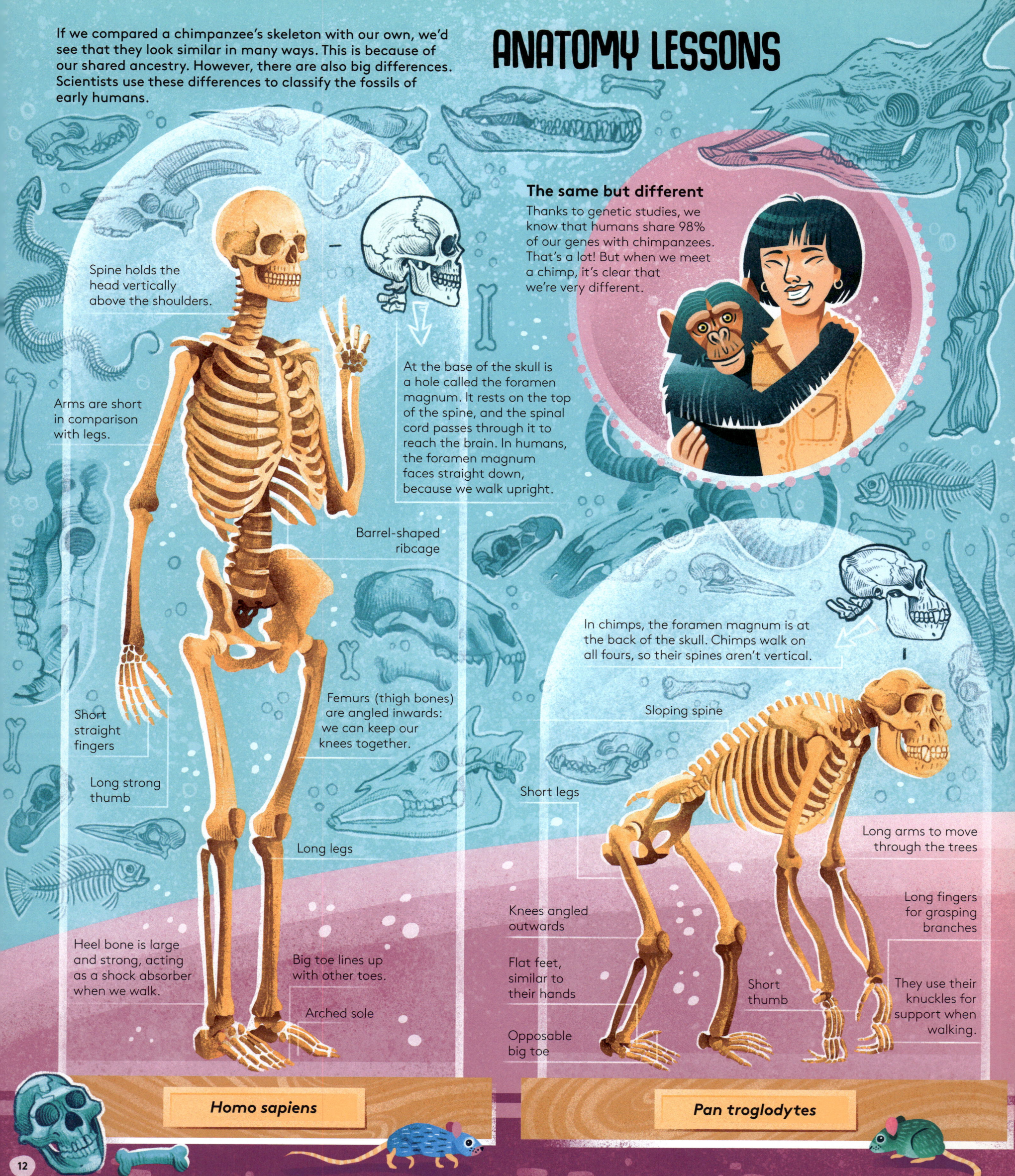

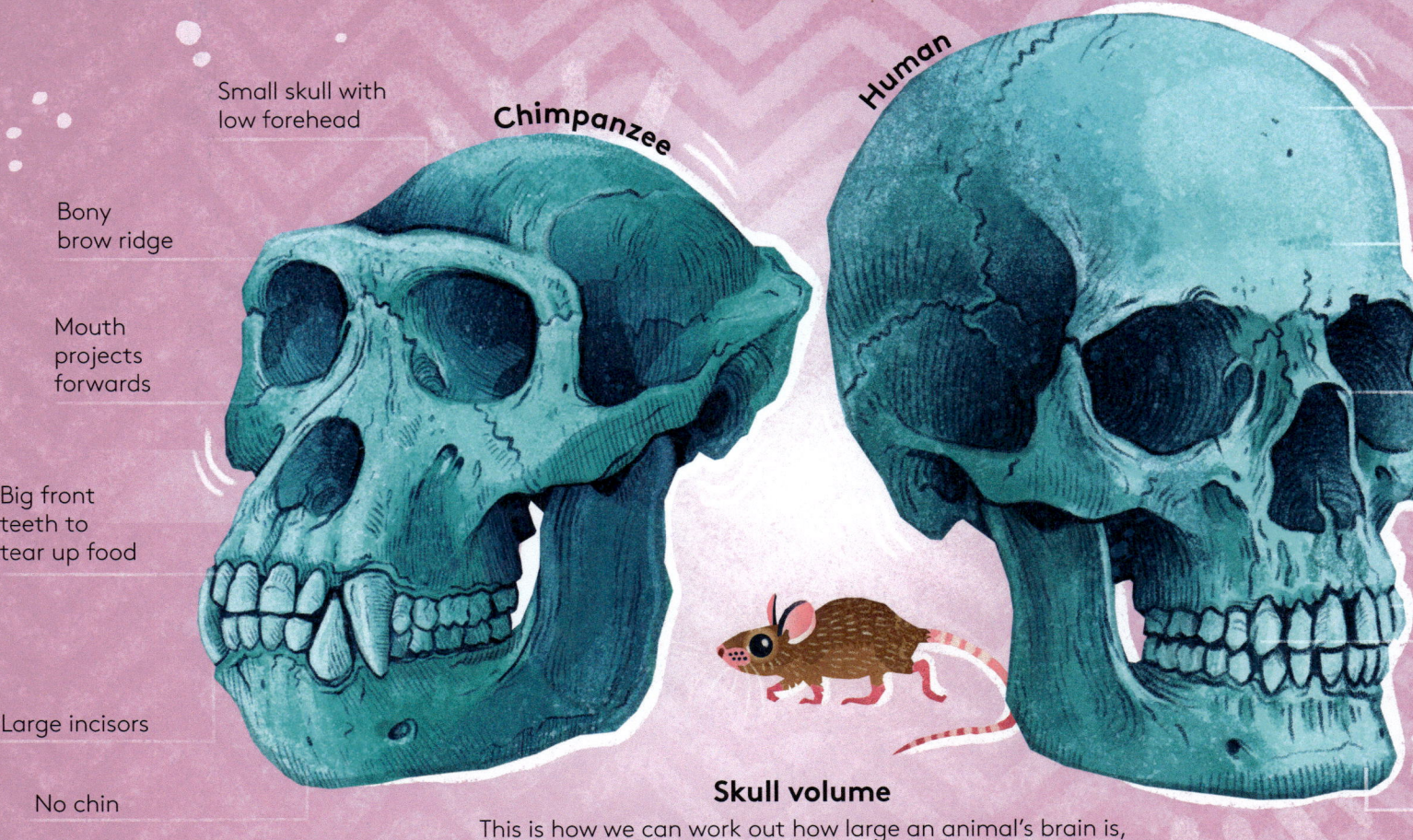

Chimpanzee
- Small skull with low forehead
- Bony brow ridge
- Mouth projects forwards
- Big front teeth to tear up food
- Large incisors
- No chin

Human
- Large and rounded skull
- Flat face with high, straight forehead
- Nasal bones that make our noses stick out
- Smaller teeth, due to our omnivore diet
- Small incisors
- The only species with a definite chin

Skull volume
This is how we can work out how large an animal's brain is, and so find out how intelligent they are. The average volume of a chimpanzee's skull is between 300 and 500 cm^3. For a human skull, it's around 1,400 cm^3.

Big brain, small pelvis
When humans became bipeds, our pelvises evolved to become narrower, while our skulls began to grow larger. This made giving birth more difficult. Evolution has solved this problem, however: human babies are born with skulls that are softer and not yet completely formed, so they can pass through the birth canal.

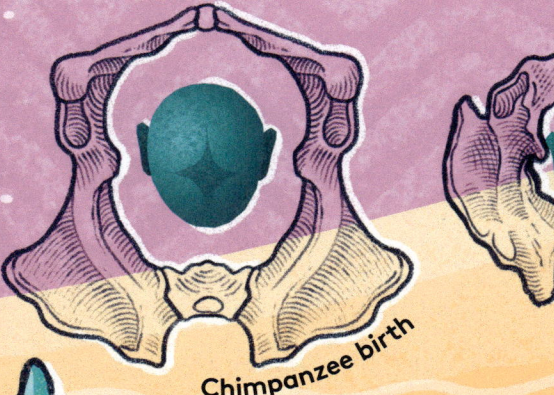

Chimpanzee birth — *Human birth*

Chimpanzee
Broad and deep pelvis. The hip bones are angled towards the back, which makes chimps sway from side to side when they walk.

Human
Shorter and narrower pelvis. The hip bones are angled to the sides, which helps to keep us stable when we walk.

A giant step for humankind
Moving around on two legs was a very important stage in human evolution. It has big advantages, but also some drawbacks. Here are a few of them.

Pros:
- Easy to make and use tools.
- It's easier to look after our children.
- Our hands are free to carry food and other objects.
- Our field of vision is raised.
- Less exposure to the sun, helping us to control our body temperature.
- We use less energy when we move around.

Cons:
- We can't run as fast as four-legged animals can.
- We are more clumsy.
- A narrow pelvis makes it harder to give birth.

WHERE IT ALL BEGAN

Our journey begins in Ethiopia, in East Africa, where we meet Ardi, a female of the species *Ardipithecus ramidus*. Her discovery was particularly important because she is the oldest known skeleton of a human ancestor. It is estimated that she lived around 4.4 million years ago.

120 cm

Ardi was found in the Afar region of northern Ethiopia.

Hairy and short, Ardi and her species had similar brains to chimpanzees, long arms for climbing trees, and feet that looked a lot like hands, with a separated big toe.

Note: The yellowish parts of this skeleton are the fragments of Ardi that have been discovered.

Ardipithecus ramidus
'Ardi' (ARA-VP-6/500)

And who are you?

When new human fossils are discovered, the first thing scientists do is compare them with the bones of other early hominins to find out what species they belong to. If they don't find anything similar, they create a new species, and give it a Latin-based scientific name.

Ardi's habitat

In the past, the landscape of East Africa was very different from today. The *Ardipithecus* species lived in dense and humid forests where they could find fruit, insects, leaves and tender shoots to feed on.

Deinotherium

STANDING TALL

Around 4 million years after Ardi, new branches began to appear on the evolutionary tree. A new genus appeared: *Australopithecus*, whose name means 'southern ape'. Members of this genus are known as australopithecines. Living in eastern and southern Africa, australopithecines were a lot like other apes, with a short stature, small brain and relatively long arms. However, they were bipeds that lived in the forests and savannah woodlands, enjoying a diet rich in leaves, fruits, small animals and insects.

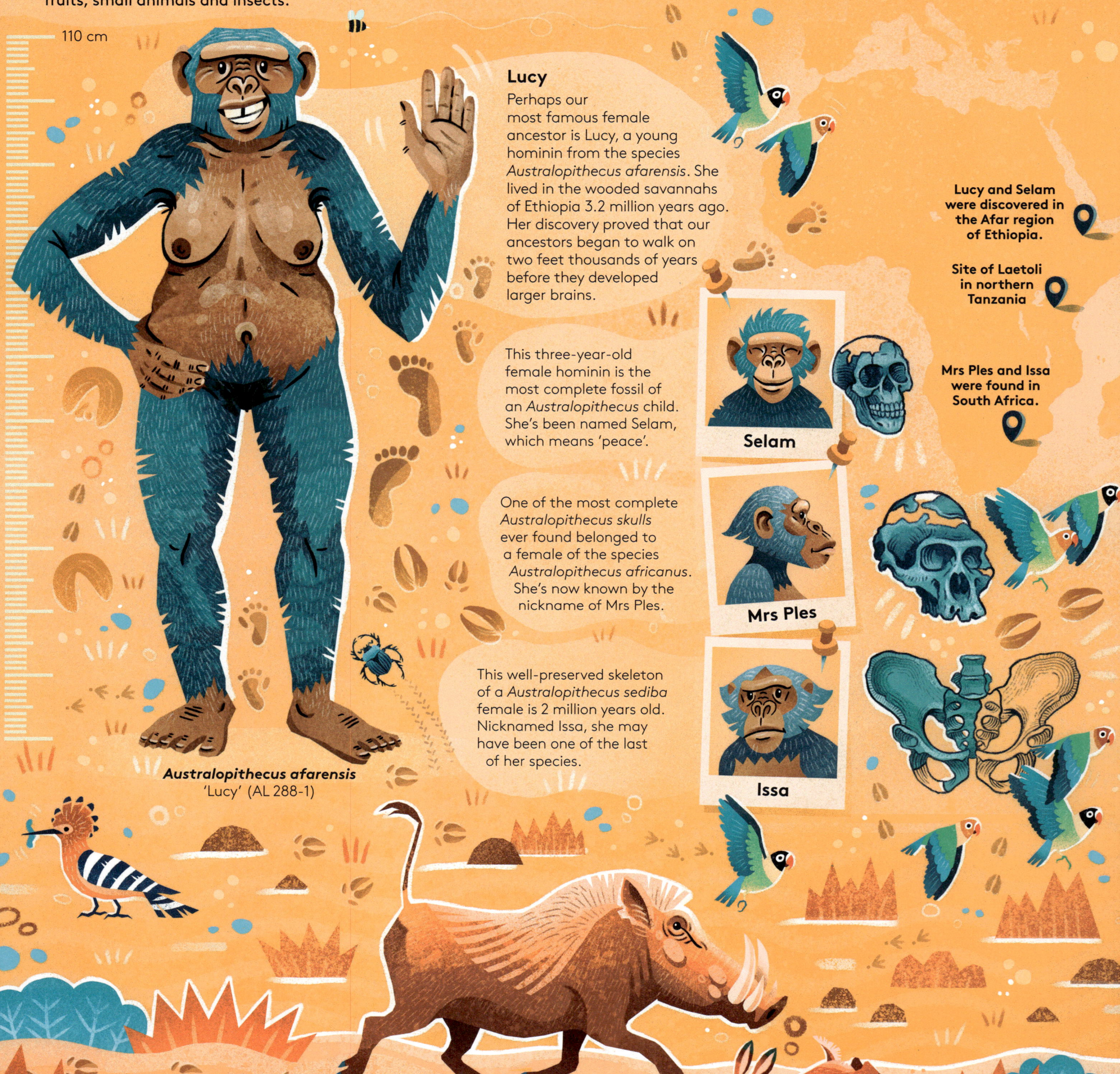

110 cm

Australopithecus afarensis
'Lucy' (AL 288-1)

Lucy
Perhaps our most famous female ancestor is Lucy, a young hominin from the species *Australopithecus afarensis*. She lived in the wooded savannahs of Ethiopia 3.2 million years ago. Her discovery proved that our ancestors began to walk on two feet thousands of years before they developed larger brains.

This three-year-old female hominin is the most complete fossil of an *Australopithecus* child. She's been named Selam, which means 'peace'.

Selam

One of the most complete *Australopithecus* skulls ever found belonged to a female of the species *Australopithecus africanus*. She's now known by the nickname of Mrs Ples.

Mrs Ples

This well-preserved skeleton of a *Australopithecus sediba* female is 2 million years old. Nicknamed Issa, she may have been one of the last of her species.

Issa

Lucy and Selam were discovered in the Afar region of Ethiopia.

Site of Laetoli in northern Tanzania

Mrs Ples and Issa were found in South Africa.

Footprint trails

Around 3.6 million years ago, a group of *Australopithecus* were walking across the savannah, through ash from a nearby volcano. When it rained, they left footprints in the wet ash. Over time, the prints were covered by volcanic rock and preserved. These footprints, found at Laetoli in northern Tanzania, show that *Australopithecus* walked upright and had similar feet to ours, with a big toe that was parallel to the others.

Chimpanzee footprint

Human footprint

Australopithecus footprint (Laetoli)

Lots of other animals also left footprints in the ash, ranging from giraffes and rhinoceroses to tiny beetles.

ADAPT OR DIE

Around 2.5 million years ago, the Earth's climate began to change dramatically. The dense woods and rainforests where *Australopithecus* lived were replaced by the dry savannah that can still be found in East Africa. The animals there had to adapt to survive, and our ancestors were no exception.

Paranthropus

Similar to *Australopithecus*, but with a stronger, sturdier body, the hominin species *Paranthropus* lived in the small pockets of woodland that still existed in eastern and southern Africa, until the species died out a million years ago.

Machairodus

Grinding machines

The changing climate meant there were fewer soft and easily chewable plants to eat, with soft fruits and tender leaves. So *Paranthropus* developed strong jaws that could deal with tougher and more fibrous plants, like tubers, roots, seeds and grass.

This change of diet gave them a more rugged appearance. Their strong jaw muscles meant they could spend hours chewing and their molars were twice as large and broad as ours, allowing them to grind up their food.

Hominin newcomers

While the *Paranthropus* genus were living in the woods and shrubland, new hominins appeared on the scene. Adventurous and daring, early members of the genus *Homo* decided to leave behind the protection of the forest and make their lives on the African savannah.

As gatherers, scavengers and hunters, they began to eat more meat, which helped their brains to develop. Their arms were shorter in relation to their bodies, and their hands were more like ours, with a strong, thick thumb.

Homo habilis
'Twiggy' (OH 24)

Female who died 1.8 million years ago

Sivatherium

Sharpened stones

The *Homo* genus made clever use of what nature provided. They began to make stone tools around 2.6 million years ago, when they discovered that hitting one piece of flint against another created a sharp edge. These flints were the first knives in history!

What makes us human?

Creating and using tools helped members of the genus *Homo* to grow more intelligent. Over time, they developed complex minds, filled with ideas. These ideas grew and became a culture, which is a key feature of humanity.

DISCOVERING NEW PLACES

Around 2 million years later, we meet another important ancestor. Members of the species *Homo ergaster* had tall, slim bodies, although their faces were still ape-like. They spread throughout Africa and beyond, before becoming extinct.

Turkana Boy
The best-known *Homo ergaster* fossil is the skeleton of a boy aged between 8 and 13. He was discovered near Lake Turkana in Kenya, so he's known as 'Turkana Boy'. This find proved that *Homo ergaster* could grow up to 1.70 metres tall and had a highly developed brain.

Out of Africa
Our ancestors were nomads, which means that they didn't always live in the same place. They moved from one area to another, searching for food and shelter. Some early human groups left the continent of Africa for the first time.

A tool revolution
This was the period when early humans started inventing more complex tools. One of the most important was the handaxe, an almond-shaped piece of flint, shaped on both sides. This multipurpose tool could be used to dig for roots, or pound bones with its long cutting edge. You could think of it as a prehistoric Swiss army knife!

Homo ergaster
'Turkana Boy' or 'Nariokotome Boy'
(KNM-WT 15000)

Starting fires
It is possible that *Homo ergaster* could make and use fire. This was a vital step. Fire not only allowed early humans to stay warm, cook food and create light, but also helped them to build social bonds and improve their technology.

Pelorovis

Who were the first to leave Africa?
Some of the earliest human remains outside Africa were found at a place called Dmanisi, in the country of Georgia. They are 1.8 million years old.

Moving on
Over time, *Homo ergaster* spread from region to region, eventually reaching Asia and evolving into a new species known as *Homo erectus*.

THE FIRST EUROPEANS

The province of Burgos in northern Spain is home to one of the world's biggest archaeological sites: the Atapuerca Mountains. This place is like a time capsule, because different human species lived in the same relatively small area for over a million years.

Unexpected discoveries

Every summer, the landscape of Atapuerca echoes with the sounds of picks, chisels and brushes. These archaeological sites have produced some amazing finds. In 1994, the remains of a number of young humans were discovered in a cave called Gran Dolina. These fossils were classified as a new species: *Homo antecessor*.

Suspicious marks
Surprisingly, all the bones found at this site were broken and had cut marks on their surfaces. These marks could only have been made by other humans using stone knives. This was the earliest known case of cannibalism.

Atapuerca Mountains

The Girl of Gran Dolina
One of the best-known remains found at this site is a piece of jawbone. At first, its owner was nicknamed 'The Boy of Gran Dolina'. But more recent studies have shown that the jawbone actually belonged to a girl, who was around ten years old.

Homo antecessor
'Girl of Gran Dolina'
(ATD6-15 & ATD6-69)

Around 850,000 years ago, *Homo antecessor* lived in this region, alongside hippopotamuses, sabre-toothed cats, mammoths, hyenas and rhinoceroses.

Unknown *Homo* species
A fragment of jawbone found at the Sima del Elefante ('Elephant Pit') in Atapuerca is estimated to be 1.2 million years old.

A FAMILY PORTRAIT

More than 400,000 years ago, the pre-Neanderthals (*Homo heidelbergensis*) lived in the Atapuerca Mountains. They looked similar to us, but they were stronger and stockier. They hunted bison and other animals, but it's likely that they ate a lot of plants and fruits too.

The Pit of Bones
This is one of the most famous archaeological sites in Atapuerca. Thousands of wonderfully preserved bones have been found here. The bodies of around thirty people were thrown into this pit after their death. This might be the earliest evidence of a prehistoric burial.

'Excalibur' handaxe
The only tool found in the Pit of Bones

Ancient DNA
The Pit of Bones is where the oldest known human DNA was found. It shows that these people were the direct ancestors of the Neanderthals.

A beloved girl
Among the human remains found here was a small skull. It belonged to a girl who was born with a disability. Nicknamed 'Benjamina', she survived to the age of around ten, so her family must have cared for and protected her until then.

Benjamina

Hunting
We know that the pre-Neanderthals were very social because they worked together in groups to hunt bison.

A group of equals
The pre-Neanderthals of Atapuerca used their mouths like a third hand, gripping pieces of meat between their teeth then cutting them with a sharp stone blade. This action has left small marks on their teeth, which show that most pre-Neanderthals were right-handed, and that both men and women did the same sorts of daily activities.

Several Atapuerca fossils show that the pre-Neanderthals cared for injured and less able members of their group.

SIBERIAN COUSINS

The Denisova cave lies in the Altai Mountains, in southern Siberia. The cold climate there has helped to preserve a very rare treasure: ancient DNA.

Meet the Denisovans

Only a few teeth and tiny bone fragments have been found at Denisova, so it's not possible to work out what these early humans looked like. However, since the fossils contain genetic material, scientists have discovered that the remains are neither from Neanderthals nor from *Homo sapiens*. This new species is now called the Denisovans, after the cave they were found in.

The Denisovans lived in the cold regions of Asia between 200,000 and 40,000 years ago. They seem to have been close relatives of the Neanderthals, with the two species even existing together at the same time.

Lasting traces

The modern-day people of Southeast Asia and Oceania still have a small percentage of Denisovan DNA, meaning their ancestors mixed with Denisovan populations thousands of years ago.

Denny the hybrid girl

One of the Denisova bone fragments tells a fascinating story. It belonged to a thirteen-year-old girl who lived around 90,000 years ago, who had a Neanderthal mother and a Denisovan father. Her DNA tells us that she may have had dark eyes, dark hair and dark skin.

NEANDERTHAL LIVES

It's time to meet the closest relatives to modern humans: the Neanderthals. Their fossils were first discovered in the early 19th century, but it was several decades before they were recognized as another species, different to our own.

Homo neanderthalensis

The Neanderthals first appeared in Europe around 300,000 years ago, spreading across the continent until they became extinct, 35,000 years ago. They were shorter and stockier than us, their bodies adapted to the cold climate of the Pleistocene ice ages. Their heads were large and long in shape, with larger brains than ours.

Neanderthal

Homo sapiens

Aurochs

Capercaillie

Like their ancestors from the Pit of Bones, the Neanderthals used their teeth to grip meat, animal hides and plant fibres. It's possible that men and women performed different tasks, as the marks found on their teeth are different from each other.

A community with their own culture

The Neanderthals invented their own technology. As well as flints, they used shells and animal bones to make tools and objects they used to decorate their bodies.

They formed small family groups, living in caves and outdoor camps where they carried out their daily activities. They buried their dead loved ones and were expert hunter-gatherers, even understanding the medicinal benefits of certain plants. They all had varied diets, and those who lived on the coast ate shellfish and other sea animals.

The Neanderthal Genome Project

In 2013, scientists extracted DNA from Neanderthal bones. It revealed that some of them had pale skin and red hair. They were able to use language and, most surprisingly of all, humans today still have some Neanderthal DNA.

UNSOLVED MYSTERIES

Sometimes fossils are discovered that change everything we think we know about the past and our ancestors. This was what happened following the discovery of the two species you are about to meet.

A new combination

Imagine putting several hominin species into a pot and giving it a good stir. What would you get? Perhaps something similar to *Homo naledi*, a human ancestor discovered at the Rising Star caves in South Africa. They had a similar body and brain to *Australopithecus*, but with a more human face. Their hands were also more like those of present-day humans so they could handle objects like we can.

Homo naledi
'Leti', a child between 4 and 6 years old.

With this unusual combination of ancient and modern features, the scientific team thought this species must have lived alongside the earliest *Homo* species, 2 million years ago. Surprisingly, however, it was found that they lived between 335,000 and 235,000 years ago – in other words, at the same time as the Neanderthals and early *Homo sapiens*!

Rising Star caves

Early *Homo sapiens* camp

Cavern with *Homo naledi* remains

Narrow passageways

Underground astronauts

Rising Star Cave 5:00

We need perhaps three or four individuals with excellent archaeological/palaeontological and excavation skills for a short-term project… The catch is this – the person must be skinny and preferably small.

An ad was posted on social media to find people who could crawl through the narrow Rising Star cave system, in order to dig up and remove the *Homo naledi* fossils. Lots of people applied, and six young women were chosen for the job. They were nicknamed the 'underground astronauts'.

Small but perfect

On the other side of the Indian Ocean, on an island called Flores in Indonesia, a team of researchers discovered the remains of the early humans that lived in this remote place between 100,000 and 50,000 years ago. This find caused a stir among scientists because *Homo floresiensis* seemed to be a much smaller version of a modern human. No one had ever heard of hominins like these, and they were nicknamed 'hobbits'.

Flo, or the Lady of Flores

The most complete skeleton from this species is an adult female who was just over one metre tall, weighed around 25 kg and whose brain size was similar to a chimpanzee's. How did these little people end up here? Did they ever come into contact with *Homo sapiens*? We don't yet know the answers.

Homo floresiensis
'Flo' (LB1)

Size matters!

Homo floresiensis shared the island with dwarf elephants, giant rats and Komodo dragons. How did this come about? Well, living on a small island means less space, fewer resources and not as many predators. In evolution terms, that means that big animals tend to grow smaller, while small animals get bigger.

Nomadic groups

Caves and rocky outcrops were used as shelters and to bury the dead. Camps were also built in the open air, made up of large huts lined with animal hides and branches. As they moved around, different groups would meet and exchange knowledge, objects and foods from other places.

Working together

Early *Homo sapiens* lived in groups of several families. Pregnant women, children and older people would work together on tasks such as gathering, hunting small animals and preparing food. The rest of the group would do tasks that required more physical strength.

THE GREAT EXPANSION

As other ancestors had done before them, groups of early *Homo sapiens* left Africa and settled in a wide variety of environments and remote places. But when did these long journeys begin?

In search of new adventures

Around 100,000 years ago, modern humans crossed the Middle East and spread south across Asia, mixing with Neanderthal and Denisovan groups on the way.

Around 20,000 years ago, when the last ice age ended and the ice sheets began to shrink, our ancestors crossed from Asia into North America, via the Bering land bridge, which no longer exists.

No more megafauna

Before *Homo sapiens* arrived in the Americas, the continent was home to a great number of large animals: mammoths, mastodons, huge sloths, sabre-toothed cats, lions, bison and giant deer, among others. After modern humans settled in these lands and the ice age ended, lots of these species went extinct, often because of hunting.

The last ice age

During the last ice age, huge ice sheets covered large areas of the world's oceans, making the sea levels drop. This meant that humans could walk between areas of land that are now separated by water.

This migration took them along the coasts towards Australia, where they probably arrived around 50,000 years ago. Homo sapiens first arrived in Europe around 50,000 years ago too, despite it being much closer to Africa.

CREATIVE MINDS

Traditionally, scientists believed that only *Homo sapiens* were capable of thinking creatively. But although it is difficult to work out when the first art appeared, there is evidence to suggest other early human species could be creative too.

Images of women's bodies have been found carved and painted on the walls of many caves.

Neanderthal art
The Neanderthals used coloured pigments, shells, and animal bones and teeth to decorate their bodies. Those living in southern Europe took feathers and claws from birds of prey and wore them as decorations.

Neanderthal ornaments from Grotte du Renne, France (40,000 y/o)

Female figures
Women played an important role in prehistoric communities. Art representing women was common, and carved female figures have been found at several sites in Europe.

Venus of Lespugue
France, 25,000 y/o

Venus of Willendorf
Austria, 25,000 y/o

Venus of Dolní Věstonice
Czechia, 29,000 y/o

Venus of Kostenki
Russia, 24,000 y/o

Venus of Renancourt
France, 23,000 y/o

Women artists?
Men were not the only ones who painted caves and created art. By studying the length of the fingers on painted handprints, experts have worked out that most of them were made by women and children.

Decorated bodies
Early *Homo sapiens* decorated their bodies with pigments, shells and beads. We know this from burial sites. For example, the so-called 'Lady of Cavillon' was buried wearing a headdress made of shells and deer teeth and was painted with red ochre.

BEYOND DEATH

Our ancient ancestors developed a wide range of burial practices. These burial sites can now provide us with lots of important information.

Vedbaek

Sunghir

Teshik Tash

Homo neanderthalensis 'Teshik-Tash 1', 8 years old

Neanderthal burials

Many Neanderthal graves have been found deep inside caves. In some cases, offerings were left beside the body.

One of the most striking examples was found at the Teshik Tash cave in Uzbekistan. The body of an eight-year-old boy was laid on a bed of horse bones, covered with flowers and surrounded by carefully placed goat's horns.

Death among *Homo sapiens*

Like the Neanderthals, early *Homo sapiens* often buried their dead inside caves, although open-air graves have also been found. The bodies of the dead are sometimes decorated with ivory or bone beads, animal teeth and body paint.

In Vedbaek, Denmark, 6,000 years ago, a woman was buried with her newborn baby, cradled on the wing of a swan.

A grave mistake

In the past, skeletons found buried with valuable offerings or weapons were often thought to be men, perhaps warriors or leaders. Studies have now shown that many of these graves belonged to women, proving that they played a vital role in ancient communities.

At the Sunghir archaeological site in Russia, several graves have been found, including the graves of two teenagers whose bodies were painted with red ochre. They were buried with lots of offerings, including ivory beads, mammoth tusks, fox teeth and carved figures.

SETTLED LIVES

The Pleistocene epoch was followed by the Holocene, which started 11,700 years ago. The last ice age ended, and *Homo sapiens* began to use their understanding of the environment to grow their own food.

The first farmers
The Holocene epoch brought warmer temperatures, and humans began to domesticate animals. Farming began in various places around the world and completely changed the human way of life.

Wolves were the first animals to be domesticated. They eventually became the pet dogs that live with lots of us today.

Jobs for everyone
As farming and animal rearing became widespread, men and women seem to have taken on jobs that were different, but equally important. Historians think women were more closely linked with making cloth and milling grain. However, this does not mean that activities like hunting were done only by men. Tasks such as preparing food, raising children and caring for others are vital to the survival of communities, and it is very likely that women played a key role in them.

Equal roles

In some present-day hunter-gatherer societies, there are no gender roles. One example is the Aka people, a nomadic community in Central Africa. Men spend half their time looking after the children, while the women go out to hunt.

Women in power

Found in a tomb in Spain, the 'Lady of Baza' is the name given to a urn decorated with the bust of a woman, and containing her ashes. The urn was buried with rich offerings (including weapons and knives) that imply a high rank. Another powerful woman was Hatshepsut, one of the few women to become a pharaoh in Ancient Egypt.

INSPIRING WOMEN

Like in many other fields of science, archaeology and the study of the human past were once entirely dominated by men. So this journey ends by paying tribute to the women pioneers who defied tradition and showed us another way to look at our history.

Jane Goodall, Dian Fossey & Biruté Galdikas

These primatologists, nicknamed the 'Trimates', dedicated their lives to observing and protecting primates in the wild. Fossey (1932–85) studied the gorillas of Rwanda, Goodall (born 1934) is a chimpanzee specialist, and Galdikas (born 1946) is an expert on orangutans. Their work has played a vital role in the study of human evolution.

Jane Dieulafoy (1851–1916)

This French explorer and archaeologist travelled the world documenting and writing about the places she visited. She often dressed like a man in order to travel more freely. Her excavation and cataloguing methods inspired other archaeologists including Howard Carter, the man who discovered the tomb of Tutankhamun.

Encarnación Cabré (1911–2005)

Considered the first woman archaeologist in Spain, she fought to protect her country's heritage during the Spanish Civil War. She combined her field work with teaching and used photography to record her research.

Dorothy Liddell (1890–1938)

Although she had no training in archaeology, she worked at many British sites, unearthing the prehistory of the UK. She was also a mentor to Mary Leakey.

Mary Leakey (1913–96)

This British archaeologist spent her life working in East Africa, where she discovered several important hominin fossils. These included the first remains of *Paranthropus boisei* and the famous Laetoli footprints.

Margaret Murray (1863–1963)
Considered the first female Egyptologist, she was also the first woman to become a lecturer in archaeology in the UK. Among other achievements, she was the first woman to publicly unwrap an Egyptian mummy.

Mary Kingsley (1862–1900)
Keen to explore the world, she defied Victorian society's strict rules. She travelled alone to Africa to learn about its people and supported the rights of African communities. She always wore a long gown when travelling and once scared away a crocodile by hitting it on the nose with a boat paddle!

Marija Gimbutas (1921–94)
Lithuanian archaeologist who studied early settlements in Europe and believed in the existence of early matriarchal societies (led by women). She combined archaeology with linguistics and the history of religion, using them in her work on the Indo-European peoples and their language.

Annette Laming-Emperaire (1917–77)
French archaeologist who brought new ideas to the study of prehistoric cave paintings. She also worked on sites in South America, and unearthed the earliest human remains ever found there.

Kathleen Kenyon (1906–78)
British archaeologist, known for leading the excavation of the city of Jericho and for her work on Neolithic communities. She helped to develop an excavation technique based on a grid of squares, known as the Wheeler-Kenyon method.

Honor Frost (1917–2010)
A pioneer in the field of underwater archaeology and a skilled illustrator. She led excavations in the Mediterranean and also a survey of the site of the ancient Lighthouse of Alexandria, finding its undersea remains.

OUR FAMILY ALBUM

Over the years, scientists have discovered around thirty different species that form part of the group of primates who came down from the trees to walk on two legs. We are the only surviving branch on that family tree.

Ardipithecus ramidus
- **Meaning:** 'Ground-root ape'
- **Sites:** Aramis, in the Awash River valley (Ethiopia)
- **Period:** 4.4–4.3 Ma (Ma = million years ago)
- **Skull volume:** 300–370 cm³
- **Height:** 1.20 m
- **Weight:** 40–50 kg
- **Habitat:** woods & rainforests
- **Home region:** East Africa

Australopithecus afarensis
- **Meaning:** 'Southern ape from the Afar region'
- **Sites:** Laetoli (Tanzania), Hadar, Maka, Omo (Ethiopia), Koobi Fora (Kenya)
- **Period:** 3.9–3 Ma
- **Skull volume:** 400–550 cm³
- **Height:** 1.50 m (male); 1 m (female)
- **Weight:** 45 kg (male); 30 kg (female)
- **Habitat:** woodlands & grasslands
- **Home region:** East Africa

Australopithecus africanus
- **Meaning:** 'Southern ape of Africa'
- **Sites:** Sterkfontein, s, Taung (South Africa)
- **Period:** 3.3–2 Ma
- **Skull volume:** 400–550 cm³
- **Height:** 1.40 m (male); 1.10 m (female)
- **Weight:** 41 kg (male); 30 kg (female)
- **Habitat:** subtropical forest
- **Home region:** Southern Africa

Paranthropus robustus
- **Meaning:** 'Robust ape that lived alongside humans'
- **Sites:** Kromdraai, Swartkrans, Drimolen (South Africa)
- **Period:** 2–1.2 Ma
- **Skull volume:** 500–550 cm³
- **Height:** 1.35 m (male); 1.10 m (female)
- **Weight:** 40 kg (male); 30 kg (female)
- **Habitat:** open woodland
- **Home region:** Southern Africa

Paranthropus boisei
- **Meaning:** 'Living alongside humans, named after Charles Boise'
- **Sites:** Olduvai (Tanzania), Konso (Ethiopia), Koobi Fora, Chesowanja (Kenya)
- **Period:** 2.3–1.2 Ma
- **Skull volume:** 475–550 cm³
- **Height:** 1.35 m (male); 1.20 m (female)
- **Weight:** 50 kg (male); 34 kg (female)
- **Habitat:** open woodland & grasslands
- **Home region:** East Africa

Homo habilis
- **Meaning:** 'Skilled human'
- **Sites:** Olduvai (Tanzania), Omo, Hadar (Ethiopia), Koobi Fora (Kenya), Sterkfontein (South Africa)
- **Period:** 2.3–1.6 Ma
- **Skull volume:** 600–700 cm³
- **Height:** 1.10–1.30 m
- **Weight:** 35–40 kg
- **Habitat:** savannah
- **Home region:** East and Southern Africa

Homo ergaster
- **Meaning:** 'Working human'
- **Sites:** Konso (Ethiopia), Koobi Fora, Nariokotome (Kenya), Swartkrans (South Africa)
- **Period:** 1.8–1 Ma
- **Skull volume:** 700–1,000 cm³
- **Height:** 1.50–1.75 m
- **Weight:** 50–70 kg
- **Habitat:** savannah
- **Home region:** East and Southern Africa

Homo antecessor
- **Meaning:** 'Pioneer human'
- **Sites:** Atapuerca (Spain)
- **Period:** 900–800 Ka (thousand years ago)
- **Skull volume:** 1,000–1,200 cm³
- **Height:** 1.60–1.85 m
- **Weight:** 60–90 kg
- **Habitat:** woodland & grasslands
- **Home region:** Southern Europe

Homo heidelbergensis (pre-Neanderthal)
- **Meaning:** 'Human from Heidelberg'
- **Sites:** Atapuerca (Spain), Mauer, Steinheim (Germany), Boxgrove, Swanscombe (UK), Petralona (Greece), Arago, Le Lazaret (France)
- **Period:** 700–200 Ka
- **Skull volume:** 1,100–1,400 cm³
- **Height:** 1.60–1.85 m
- **Weight:** 50–90 kg
- **Habitat:** steppes, grasslands & woods
- **Home region:** Europe

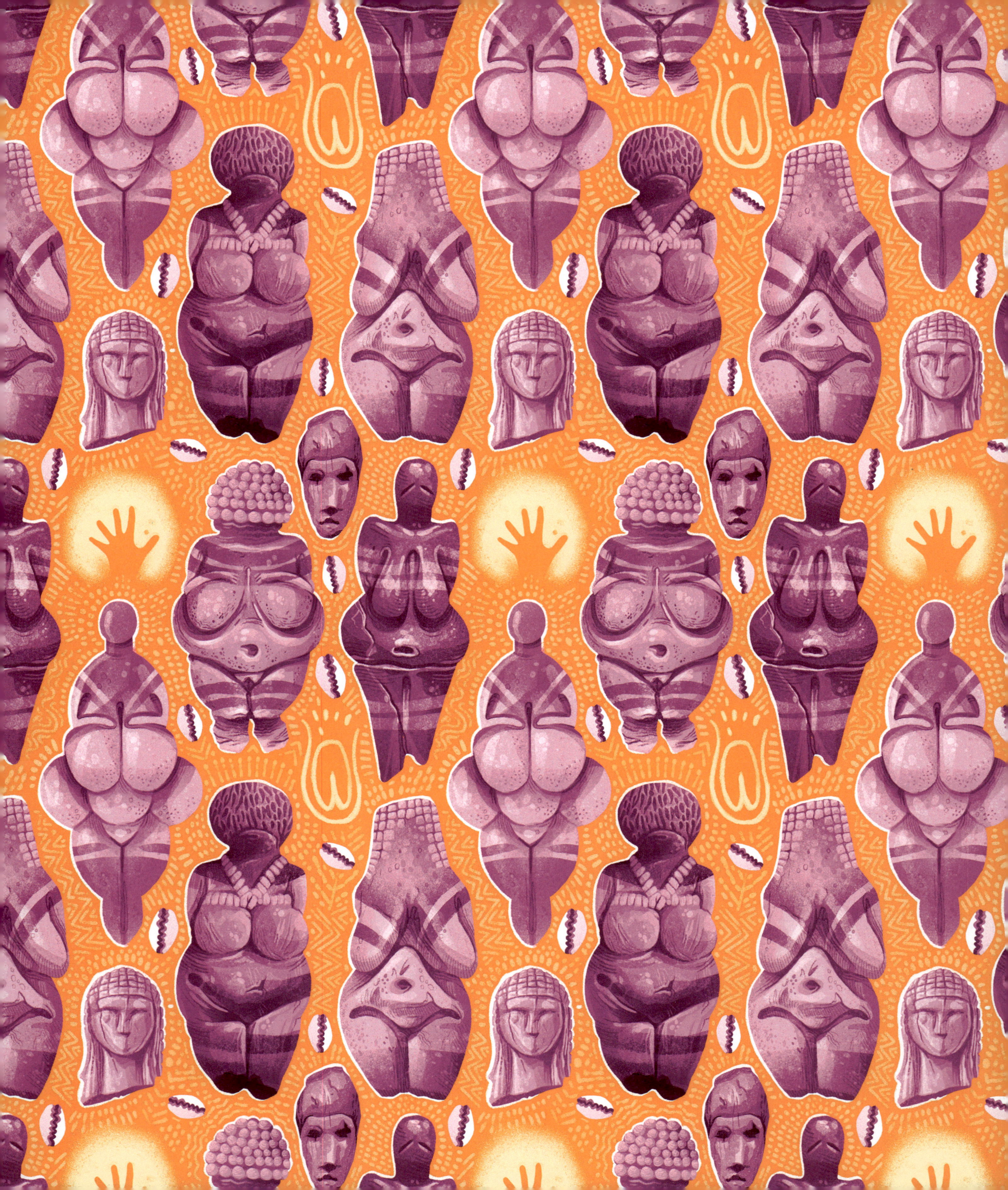